AF228910

US ARMED FORCES

UNITED STATES
COAST GUARD

KENNY ABDO

Fly!
An Imprint of Abdo Zoom
abdobooks.com

abdobooks.com

Published by Abdo Zoom, a division of ABDO, P.O. Box 398166, Minneapolis, Minnesota 55439. Copyright © 2019 by Abdo Consulting Group, Inc. International copyrights reserved in all countries. No part of this book may be reproduced in any form without written permission from the publisher. Fly!™ is a trademark and logo of Abdo Zoom.

Printed in the United States of America, North Mankato, Minnesota.
092018
012019

Photo Credits: Alamy, iStock, Shutterstock, US Coast Guard, US Navy
Production Contributors: Kenny Abdo, Jennie Forsberg, Grace Hansen
Design Contributors: Dorothy Toth, Neil Klinepier

Library of Congress Control Number: 2018946312

Publisher's Cataloging-in-Publication Data

Names: Abdo, Kenny, author.
Title: United States Coast Guard / by Kenny Abdo.
Description: Minneapolis, Minnesota : Abdo Zoom, 2019 | Series: US Armed
     Forces | Includes online resources and index.
Identifiers: ISBN 9781532125522 (lib. bdg.) | ISBN 9781641856973 (pbk) |
     ISBN 9781532126543 (ebook) | ISBN 9781532127052 (Read-to-me ebook)
Subjects: LCSH: United States. Coast Guard--Juvenile literature. | Coastal
     surveillance--Juvenile literature. | Search and rescue operations--Juvenile
     literature. | Military departments and divisions--United States--Juvenile
     literature.
Classification: DDC 363.28--dc23

TABLE OF CONTENTS

COAST GUARD

Reporting on national and international waters, the Coast Guard protects the safety and security of the United States of America.

The US Coast Guard's motto is *Semper Paratus*. It means "Always Ready" in Latin. They serve during times of both peace and war.

The Coast Guard is one of the oldest forces of the **federal government**. It was formed in 1790. It was briefly known as the Revenue Marine, then renamed the Revenue Cutter Service.

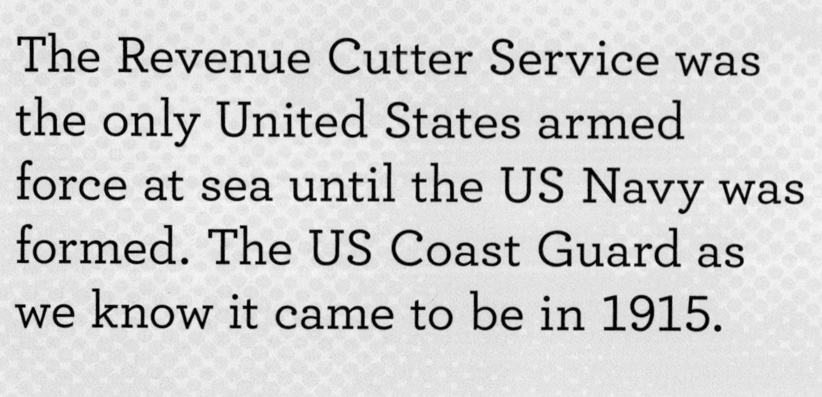

The Revenue Cutter Service was the only United States armed force at sea until the US Navy was formed. The US Coast Guard as we know it came to be in 1915.

From the beginning, the Coast Guard has served in all of the United States' wars and conflicts.

U. S. COAST GUARD

The Coast Guard protects about 100,000 miles (16,093.4 km) of US **coastline**. It also defends the largest Exclusive Economic Zone (EEZ) in the world.

This EEZ starts north of the **Arctic Circle** and goes south of the **equator**. In total, it covers 4.5 million square miles (11.6 million square km).

IN ACTION

There are more than 40,000 active duty members of the US Coast Guard. They serve all over the world, including in the Arctic, Japan, and Iraq.

The Coast Guard has many **duties**. They ensure the nation's **maritime** safety, security, and **stewardship**.

The Coast Guard responds to many search and rescue (SAR) **missions** every year. They assist about 4,000 lives.

GLOSSARY

Arctic Circle – an imaginary line that circles the North Pole at about 66° north latitude.

coastline – the outline of land near the sea.

duty – an action that an organization is tasked to perform.

equator – an imaginary circle around the middle of Earth. It is halfway between the North and South poles.

federal government – the central government of the United States.

maritime – military activity on the sea.

mission – an important job carried out by the armed forces.

stewardship – the job of taking care of something.

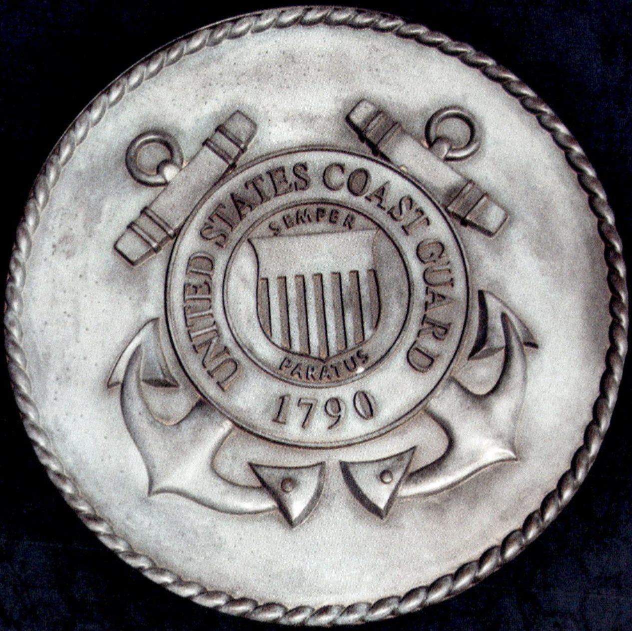

ONLINE RESOURCES

To learn more about the US Coast Guard, please visit **abdobooklinks.com**. These links are routinely monitored and updated to provide the most current information available.

INDEX